Why Good Girls go Bad

Unleashing your inner *Bad Girl*

Paige Anders

ISBN 10: **1463739982**
ISBN-13 **978-1463739980**
:

DEDICATION

To all the women who will learn that *Bad* is the new *Good*

May you live a *Badder* Life!

CONTENTS

ACKNOWLEDGMENTS

I would like to thank the students at Cal State Fullerton for allowing me to interview and interrogate them. Especially Mary and Sue who put up with me for days on end. I could not have written this without the generous help and input from Dr. Carol Schulman PHD and Randy Forester journalist for the Times. Thanks also to the Cherry Crossing Women's helpline for answering endless questions on women's behavioral issues especially to Anne. And of course last but not least my Editor for all the sleepless nights!

1

WHY GOOD GIRLS GO BAD

When a girl goes bad–men go right after her. ~ *Mae West*

Time and time again you see it happening. Seemingly good girls gone bad. By bad I mean they have shunned their moral upbringing in trade for a life they were always warned against. I'm talking about the girl in all of us that was raised to think and behave like our parents and society vehemently demanded.

We see it all the time in the tabloids. Young actresses with Disney mentalities turning to a rough and dangerous path of debauchery and excess. Drug fueled parties and bad boys in tow hitting the club scene with reckless abandon. I call it the "Party ethic". If I would have put the same commitment into an education I would have had my Master's degree. Instead I wound up with low self esteem, ill health and a general sense of self loathing. The end result is always bad but that doesn't seem to stop us from wanting to see for ourselves. I'm not saying the highs are not high but I really feel you need to weigh them against the extreme lows.

So where do these girls come from and what fuels their behavior? Are we spurning a new breed of monster by forcing our rigid teachings on our children or is it caused by the society we live in today. Women are conflicted by old traditional roles and their newly learned independent ones. We are the products of a traditional past and feminist future. A "stay weak but be strong" catch 22. Dan Kindlon, a professor of child psychology at Harvard and author of "Alpha Girls," calls these girls the daughters of the revolution, the first generation that is reaping the full benefit of the women's movement. "Sure, there are plenty of girls with big problems out there," he says. "Like the 'Girls Gone Wild' videos. But what percentage of the college population is that?" There is still plenty of pressure to be beautiful and thin, he adds, but now there are more options. Girls can define themselves as athletes or good students. For better or for worse, it may also be that they now feel entitled to dress as crassly as they choose, date unwisely and fall down drunk, the way men have since the dawn of time.

I have found a strong coinciding link to strict religious upbringing and wild rebellious behavior later in life. Take the "The Washington Post" article "Catholic Girls gone wild?" written by Patrick J. Reilly president and founder, The Cardinal Newman Society in which he states; It was not so long ago, when singer Billy Joel's chiding plea to "Come Out, Virginia" resonated with thousands of young people born into the Sexual Revolution, many of them reveling in American society's defiance of the Catholic Church and traditional sexual mores. According to a new study, Virginia may not be so reluctant anymore. Researchers from Mississippi State University considered a survey of 1,000 college students nationwide and were surprised to find that "women attending colleges and universities affiliated with the Catholic Church are almost four times as likely to have participated in 'hooking up' compared to women at secular schools."

Perhaps the Bad Girl is a portrait of our present society's perception of the modern woman. Just within the last few centuries, we've won our right to voice our opinions by voting, manage our own accounts, and own our own property. We've come a long way, and we couldn't have done it without all the Bad Girls in history who did their time and pushed the limits. America is slowly becoming more encouraging of strong, capable women who not only can raise a family, but can raise themselves up too. The age of the meek little southern Belle with impeccable manors and a speak-only-when-spoken-to demeanor is coming to a close. And sexy Miss Independent is shoving her out of the way.

Still I think the real reason bad girls get away with so much is the fact that men love them and are drawn to them like bees on honey! Even other women respect them. Bad Girls are to be reckoned with carefully. You never know what they will do next. Mystery intrigue and high drama all seem to trail her every move.

2

FAMOUS BAD GIRLS

Mae West

Mae West, Mama of the bad girl persona was born in Brooklyn 1893 to Irish Catholic immigrant parents. Hmmm, I'm sensing a pattern here. Her trademark phrases have been translated into numerous languages, including Mandarin, Mongolian, Norwegian, and Lithuanian. Encouraged by her mother, she used her sexuality to build alliances with, or dominate, nearly every man who crossed her path. And she learned to view marriage as a double edged institution – one that offered legal protection and social acceptance, but which robbed women of their independence and sexual freedom. According to most sources she took refuge in marriage just once, with fellow actor and lover Frank Wallace. She wrote and starred in bawdy theatrical productions, delighting and scandalizing audiences. She went too far, however, when she wrote a play called "Sex," about waterfront hookers and pimps, which became a national hit. In 1927, the New York production was raided and she was arrested, convicted of a performance that "tended to corrupt the morals of youth and others," and sentenced to 10 days in jail, according to The New York Times. Seven years later she was featured on the cover of NEWSWEEK for a story titled "The Churches Protest," which called her the "personification of Hollywood's sins."

Elizabeth Taylor

Perhaps the most coveted good/bad girl of all time was the legendary dame herself Elizabeth Taylor. She will always be revered as Hollywood royalty and one of the greatest actresses' of all time. Elizabeth Rosemond Taylor was born at Heathwood, in a northwestern suburb of London; the younger of two children. Her parents were originally from Kansas and brought her up in a very middle class, Bible belt fashion. She was America's sweetheart and never a word was written about any childhood dramas. It wasn't till she stole the heart of Eddy Fisher away from then wife, Debbie

Reynolds that her pure as snow reputation slighted a bit. Reminiscent of The Brad Pitt and Angelina Jolie scandal. Taylor was hounded by the press. Just as the public seemed to forgive her slightly she shocked everyone by taking up with Richard Burton whom she later married, divorced and remarried again.

The Vatican denounced her as "a woman of loose morals." When "Dickenliz," as they were known, checked into a Toronto hotel, protesters marched outside with signs that read DRINK NOT THE WINE OF ADULTERY, according to a 1964 NEWSWEEK article.

No matter what bad girl behavior Elizabeth Taylor indulged in, her star continued to rise

Madonna

When it comes to good girls gone bad Madonna could have written the book! Born in 1958 as Madonna Louise Ciccone in Bay City Michigan. She was raised as an Italian Catholic. I can relate to her more than anyone else. Similar in age and upbringing. I'm sensing a real relevance between Catholic upbringing and rebellion in adolescence. America had become harder to shock—until 1984, that is, when Madonna showed up in a wedding dress at the first MTV Video Music

Awards and sang "Like a Virgin" while gyrating on the floor. When her "Virgin" tour opened a year later, parents fretted over the hordes of Madonna wannabes who thronged her concerts dressed in tatty lace, spandex and armfuls of black rubber bracelets. The Material Girl went on to outrage both Planned Parenthood and the Catholic Church in 1986 with her single "Papa Don't Preach," about a pregnant teenager. The 1992 coffee-table book called "Sex," which glorified nearly every sexual fetish you can think of, cemented her title as the Queen of Bad Girls. Eleven years later she passed on her crown to Britney with a lingering French kiss on the stage of yet another MTV Video Music Awards ceremony.

Angelina Jolie

What Angelina wants Angelina gets! This is what poor Jen found out the hard way. To some, Angelina is a she- devil in disguise. Men want her and women want to keep their men away from her. She is regarded as one of the sexiest women alive! Born June 4th 1975 in Los Angeles, California, Jolie is the daughter of actor Jon Voight and Marcheline Bertrand. She was raised primarily by her Mother in a loving environment with her brother. She had a strained relationship with her father after he divorced her mother.

In early 2005, Jolie was involved in a well-publicized Hollywood scandal when she was accused of being the reason for the divorce of actors Brad Pitt and Jennifer Aniston. She and Pitt were alleged to have started an affair during filming of *"Mr. and Mrs. Smith"*. She denied this on several occasions, but later admitted that they "fell in love" on the set. She explained in 2005, "To be intimate with a married man, when my own father cheated on my mother, is not something I could forgive. I could not look at myself in the morning if I did that. I wouldn't be attracted to a man who would cheat on his wife." Jolie and Pitt did not publicly comment on the nature of their relationship until January 2006, when Jolie confirmed to *People Magazine* that she was pregnant with Pitt's child. The couple—dubbed "Brangelina" by the entertainment media—are the subject of worldwide media coverage.

Lindsay Lohan

Case in point, Lindsay Lohan. I find the similarities always the same. Strict religious background and always the model child starring in several Disney films. Here is the backdrop of Lindsay's past

She was born Lindsay Dee Lohan on the 2nd of July, 1986, spending her early years in Laurel Hollow, a tiny residential village on the western shore of Cold Spring Harbour, Long Island, New York. This place was a fair reflection of her Irish-Italian Catholic family's fortunes at this point. A former whaling village, it had been popularized in the early 1900s by

well-to-do New Yorkers like Louis Comfort Tiffany, son of
the founder of Tiffany's, who founded estates there. As time
passed the area became famed for its bird sanctuary, the
Mutton town Preserve woodlands and then a genetic and
cancer research centre that spawned three Nobel Prize
winners. Though just a few miles outside the New York
conurbation, it was leafy, sparsely populated and rich. Come
the year 2000 its population was still 91.3% white with a
median income of over $200,000. It was Gatsby country.

Here is a rundown on Lindsay today

 According to the Huffington post: "What Lohan says is true
-- she *is* a "damn good actress," especially when it comes to
the cycle of downward spiral followed by redemption
followed by downward spiral.

Bad behavior, apology, and then repeat.

Let's travel back in time to the summer of 2007. Fresh out of
rehab, Lohan was arrested again that July on DUI and
cocaine possession charges after a bizarre car chase. A month
later, Lohan issued a long and seemingly heartfelt apology to
TMZ after pleading guilty to seven misdemeanors.

"It is clear to me that my life has become completely
unmanageable because I am addicted to alcohol and drugs,"
the star wrote. "Recently, I relapsed and did things for which
I am ashamed. I broke the law, and today I took
responsibility by pleading guilty to the charges in my case.
No matter what I said when I was under the influence on the
day I was arrested, I am not blaming anyone else for my
conduct other than myself."

LiLo went on to vow to get "healthy" and "gain control of my
life and career" and said she sought medical help to get her

back on track.

That fall, the actress spent 84 minutes in jail before her release. But that wasn't the end of it.

Within months, she'd had her probation extended because she repeatedly failed to show up for her required substance abuse classes. And her cycle of going to clubs, getting drunk and driving under the influence continued.

In the September Vanity Fair, Lohan admits she's been a bit of a train wreck at times. But she denies abusing prescription drugs denies being an alcoholic blames her struggles on her father Michael and brushes off her entire collection of crazy antics as ordinary old growing pains".

Katy Perry

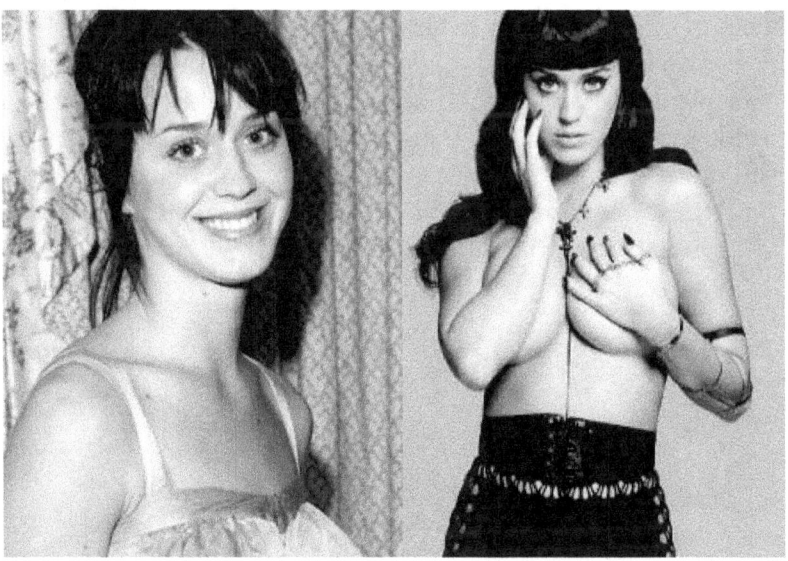

"When my daughter came out and sang that song, 'I kissed a girl, and I liked it.' I said, 'My ministry is over.'" So says Perry's father, **Keith Hudson**, a "prophet/evangelist" for the **Life Christian Church** based just north of San Diego, CA. Hudson and his wife Mary raised Katy with no television, her only entertainment being the Bible and gospel music. Mary, for her part, has also been very vocal when it comes to Katy's breakout hit. "We cannot cut her out of our lives as she is our child," she once said. "But she knows we disagree strongly with what she is doing and the message she is promoting regarding homosexuality, which the Bible clearly states is a sin." Katy's uninhibited adult persona is seen via the 26-year-old's sexually-charged lyrics, revealing costumes and marriage to wild boy **Russell Brand**, but she's managed not to alienate her parents too much; they travel around the world with her to this day. When asked about her departure from representing Christianity, she has an interesting opinion on why her music isn't as bad as say, Gaga's. "I am sensitive to Russell taking the Lord's name in vain, and to Lady Gaga putting a rosary in her mouth," she told *Rolling Stone* last year. "Yes, I said I kissed a girl. But I didn't say I kissed a girl while fucking a crucifix." And when Gaga's "Alejandro" video was released, Perry also famously tweeted: "Using blasphemy as entertainment is as cheap as a comedian telling a fart joke." But posing topless with crosses (as seen above) is perfectly okay though, right Katy?

LADY GAGA

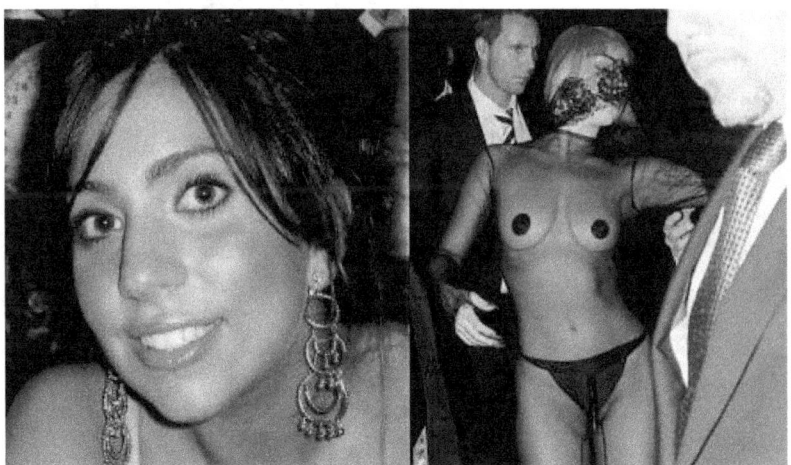

She's Madonna's heir apparent in too many ways to count, but their most glaring similarity may be that of being a young Italian-American female rebelling against their Roman Catholic upbringing. As with many Catholics, Gaga, 25, is honest in her frustration with many of the church's tenets. She once told **Larry King**, "I believe in Jesus, I believe in God, I'm very spiritual, I pray. At the same time there isn't one religion that doesn't hate or speak against or be prejudiced against another racial group or religious group or sexual group. I guess you could say I'm a very religious woman who is confused about religion." But critics have said while Madonna provoked real ire from the church for her 1989 "Like A Prayer" video (she danced in front of a burning cross, amongst other things) and invited **Pope Benedict XVI**

to watch her be crucified on stage during a 2006 Rome tour stop, Gaga's attempts to do the same have failed (*Salon* says Gaga's "Judas" video was "ultimately too confusing to upset anyone"). Can't say the girl isn't trying though; the "Alejandro" video saw her swallowing rosary beads in a latex-version of a nun's habit, holding a crucifix in front of her crotch and simulating group sex with a bunch of almost naked, beefed-up men. Her support of gay rights in unwavering; she calls the LGBT community "revolutionaries of love" and promotes "full equality now" for same-sex couples from churches and governments worldwide.

JESSICA SIMPSON

While she's definitely the tamest of the bunch, **Jessica Simpson** has enjoyed her fair share of controversy. Things definitely started off right for the Baptist-raised pop star: she was signed to a gospel label early in her career, performed on the Christian youth conference circuit and remained a virgin till she married **Nick Lachey** (her father, preacher **Joe Simpson**, even gave her a purity ring when she was 12). Originally wanting to pursue a career as a gospel artist, Jessica was reportedly knocked back by Christian record labels due to her shapely frame at a young age. "They said it could cause guys to lust," she once explained. "I didn't understand why they were passing judgment on me, especially since I walked in in overalls, nothing revealing." Her move to pop music proved lucrative, but things definitely got a little weird at times. Like when Papa Joe told *GQ* magazine, "Jessica never tries to be sexy. She just is sexy. If you put her in a T-shirt or you put her in a bustier, she's sexy in both. She's got double D's! You can't cover those suckers up!" (Joe also apparently "saved" other daughter **Ashlee** from playing a lesbian in a film role). And when Jessica covered **Nancy Sinatra**'s hit "These Boots Are Made For Walkin'" for the *Dukes of Hazzard* soundtrack, the video (where she wore teeny-tiny **Daisy Dukes** while flirting in a bar, plus writhed in a revealing pink bikini all over a car) was banned in a number of countries for its overtly sexual content. She also received criticism from Christian groups to which she responded, "It didn't really surprise me because I grew up with a lot of that backlash. That's why I didn't end up going into the Christian music industry. I think that if they're really good Christians the judgment wouldn't be there."

Brittany Spears

It seems there no sadder case of a girl gone bad than Brittany Spears. She just couldn't seem to transition well. Confusing bad girls for crazy girls. She is as well known for shaving her head and having a joke wedding in Las Vegas, as she is for her smash-hit songs and records.

Britney Spears has seen the best, and the worst, that fame has to offer. Once a teen pop icon at the height of stardom - with songs such as 'Baby One More Time' and 'Oops I did it again' - she has fallen apart at the seams and been splashed across tabloid newspapers for her protracted divorce and custody

battles with Kevin Federline; for checking in and out of
rehabilitation facilities; and for her so-so comeback tour.

Brittany has gone back to being a good girl for now. Her
father's hand at conservatorship seems to be working. She is
the classic case of someone who never should have attempted
the bad girl transformation. Some girls should just stay true
to their good girl roots. Maybe in time with some more
maturity under her belt she may surprise us all by attempting
it again and succeeding this time. We may all be humming
the tune *Ooop's she did it again.*

Jessica Rabbit

Even animated girls find it hard to be good. "I'm not bad I was just drawn that way" became a catchphrase quoted around the world. This red headed sex bomb epitomizes the joys of bringing men to their knees. Who framed Roger Rabbit may not have been the hit it was without her. I know many a man that would gladly give up reality to become a toon in her world.

Jessica Rabbit is Roger's buxom wife in the book and movie. In the book, she was an immoral, up-and-coming star and former comic character, over whom her estranged husband, comic strip star Roger Rabbit, obsessed. She is re-imagined in the film as a sultry, but moral, cartoon singer at a Los Angeles supper club called The Ink and Paint Club. She is one of several suspects in the framing of her husband, who is a famous cartoon star. She is voiced by Kathleen Turner. Amy Irving was cast to sing "Why don't you do right" (a blues song made famous by Peggy Lee) for Jessica's first scene in the movie.

Apparently Jessica wreaked Havoc long after the film wrapped proving you can't keep a bad toon down.

According to Wikipedia; Disagreements between the Walt Disney company, Amblin Entertainment (Spielberg) and Gary Wolf (jointly owning rights to the characters) made it difficult for any merchandise or projects to get off the ground and caused the halt of the short film, *Hare in My Soup*, and the next film *Who Discovered Roger Rabbit*. In this prequel, Roger meets his bride-to-be, Jessica. A completed score by Alan Silvestri is said to exist as well as test footage and computer generated versions of the characters. Also cancelled was an animated television series, which was replaced by a show called *Bonkers* about a feline cop. Many park attractions never got out of development, such as Roger Rabbit's Hollywood. In 2000, Disney-MGM Studios stopped using any character memorabilia in the park, though some props are still present. These include a Maroon Cartoon billboard featuring Roger, Jessica, and Baby Herman across from the *Indiana Jones Epic Stunt Spectacular show*, Eddie Valiant's office and a cut-out of Roger on the blinds of a neighboring window near the 50's Prime Time Cafe, and the "ton o' bricks" hanging near the "Honey, I Shrunk the Kids" Movie Set Adventure.

In 2008, Jessica Rabbit was selected by *Empire Magazine* as one of *The 100 Greatest Movie Characters of All Time*. In March, 2009, a UK newspaper voted Jessica Rabbit the sexiest cartoon character of all time, with Betty Boop in second place and the Cadbury Bunny in third.

Will animated bad girls steal the limelight from the likes of Betty Boop, Cinderella and Snow White? Will there be more animated bad girls than good girls to serve as role models in the future? I guess we will all have to stay *tooned* to find out.

Cat Woman   **Poison Ivy**

A **villain** is an "Evil" character in a story, whether a historical narrative or, especially, a work of fiction. The villain usually is the **bad guy**, the character who fights against the hero. A female villain is sometimes called a **villainess**. Random House Unabridged Dictionary defines villain as "a cruelly malicious person who is involved in or devoted to wickedness or crime; scoundrel; or a character in a play, novel, or the like, who constitutes an important evil agency in the plot."

Batman gave us our first taste of Bad girl villainesses. They personified a don't mess with me attitude while seducing men into a state of frenzy. Directly aimed at young impressionable minds it's no wonder we all were intrigued with the bad girl image. Who wants to be the helpless good girl when these superheroes were kicking ass and getting everything they wanted.

In 1950, the Cincinnati Parents Committee began rating almost all comic books published on their own criteria of art, writing, printing, and objectional content. Their ratings were published annually in Parents Magazine.

The U.S. Federal Government jumped into the fray in 1950. A U.S. Senate special committee was doing an investigation into organized crime. A part of this investigation looked into the 'effects' that crime comics had. One judge on the committee stated that he had cases where boys had committed a crime that was patterned after one depicted in a comic book. Blaming comic books for their crimes suddenly became an easy way out for kids. The kids would be given sympathy, for it was the comic book that "made them do it."

Even though there were a number of people in the media who were critical of comic books, Dr. Wertham's book Seduction of the Innocent, published in 1954, had the most devastating effects. In this book Dr. Wertham stated that in his studies with children, he found comic books to be a major cause of juvenile delinquency. This assertion was based mostly on guilt by association. The vast majority of kids in those days read comic books, including the ones who became delinquents. But according to Dr. Wertham, comic books caused the children to become delinquents. Could it stand to reason then that young girls might be corrupted into becoming like their female superhero counterparts?

Delilah   Eve

Famous 'Samson and Delilah' Baroque by Peter Paul Rubens ca. 1610

Photo: Daniel Berehulak / Getty Images

"Delilah" the biblical bad girl. Using her powers of seduction and deception, Delilah persistently wore down Samson with her repeated requests, until he finally divulged the crucial information. Having taken the Nazi rite vow at birth, Samson had been set apart to God. As part of that vow, his hair was never to be cut. When Samson told Delilah that his strength would leave him if a razor were to be used on his head, she cunningly crafted her plan with the Philistine rulers. While Samson slept on her lap, Delilah called in a co-conspirator to shave off the seven braids of his hair. Subdued and weak, Samson was captured. So you see loving bad girls' dates back to The Bible. Let us not forget about the first bad girl and woman on earth "Eve".

Eve was the first woman on earth, the first wife, and the first mother. She is known as the "Mother of All the Living." And although this is quite a remarkable accomplishment, very little is known about Eve. There is not much said of her in the book of **Geneses**. Like most mothers, even though her accomplishments were great, they were for the most part, overlooked.

Eve was **Adam**'s companion, his helper, the one who would complete him and share equally in his responsibility over **creation**. Eve was seduced by the devil in the form of a snake. She then tempted Adam with the thought of biting into the apple that God forbid them to have. It will open all knowledge to us she urged. Adam gave in and they were both banished from the Garden of Eden for all eternity.

3

WHY DO MEN LOVE BAD GIRLS?

Maybe asking why men have the desire to breathe would be more to the point. Let's explore basic animal attraction. Snips and snails and puppy dog tails that's what little boys are made of. If only it were that fanciful and easy. Here's a rundown on what they are really made up of.

Testosterone is a steroid hormone from the androgen group and is found in mammals, reptiles, birds and other vertebrates. In mammals, testosterone is primarily secreted in the testes of males and the ovaries of females, although small amounts are also secreted by the adrenal glands. It is the principal male sex hormone and an anabolic steroid.

In men, testosterone plays a key role in the development of male reproductive tissues such as the testis and prostate as well as promoting secondary sexual characteristics such as increased muscle, bone mass and the growth of body-hair. In addition, testosterone is essential for health and well-being as well as the prevention of osteoporosis.

On average, an adult human male body produces about ten times more testosterone than an adult human female body, but females are more sensitive to the hormone.

Physiological effects

In general, androgens promote protein synthesis and growth of those tissues with androgen receptors. Testosterone effects can be classified as virilizing and anabolic, although the distinction is somewhat artificial, as many of the effects can be considered both. Testosterone is anabolic, meaning it builds up bone and muscle mass.

- *Anabolic effects* include growth of muscle mass and strength, increased bone density and strength, and stimulation of linear growth and bone maturation.
- *Androgenic effects* include maturation of the sex organs, particularly the penis and the formation of the scrotum in the fetus, and after birth (usually at puberty) a deepening of the voice, growth of the beard and auxiliary hair. Many of these fall into the category of male secondary sex characteristics

Testosterone effects can also be classified by the age of usual occurrence. For postnatal effects in both males and females, these are mostly dependent on the levels and duration of circulating free testosterone.

- Falling in love decreases men's testosterone levels while increasing women's testosterone levels. It is speculated that these changes in testosterone result in the temporary reduction of differences in behavior between the sexes. It has been found that when the testosterone and endorphins in the ejaculated semen meet the cervical wall after sexual intercourse, females receive a spike in testosterone, endorphin, and oxytocin levels, and males after orgasm during copulation experience an increase in endorphins and a marked increase in oxytocin levels.

This adds to the hospitable physiological environment in the female internal reproductive tract for conceiving, and later for nurturing the conceptus in the pre-embryonic stages, and stimulates feelings of love, desire, and paternal care in the male (this is the only time male oxytocin levels rival a female's).

- Recent studies suggest that testosterone levels play a major role in risk-taking during financial decisions.
- The administration of testosterone makes men selfish and more likely to punish others for being selfish towards them.
- Fatherhood also decreases testosterone levels in men, suggesting that the resulting emotional and behavioral changes promote paternal care

So you can see when men say they can't control themselves at times, they seem to have a valid scientific reason. If you can understand how different men are from women you will have half the battle won. Women are made up of estrogen which is the opposite of testosterone. We tend to be maternal, sympathetic and emotional. The key to happiness therefore is in learning how to co exist. Women must accept, forgive and understand men's testosterone fueled behavior and men must do the same in turn for our estrogen driven follies.

Men quite simply want *SEX*, some more than others but they can't help but think about it every few seconds. Bad girls live by this knowledge and play up to men with their weakness in mind. They know how to keep their man on the edge at all times.

So what is it that men find so attractive about bad girls?

Here are some reasons given in Cosmopolitan Magazine by men who are attracted to bad girls;

1. A guy has way more leeway with a bad girl: If he has an extensive romantic past, no problem…so does she. If he has a few too many drinks with his buddies and accidentally gets arrested, it's okay — the same thing has happened to her.

2. There really aren't a whole lot of panties being worn.

3. Guys are absolutely certain that all bad girls are amazing in bed. And even if one isn't, the guy is so certain that all bad girls are amazing in bed that he convinces himself that she is.

4. A bad girl would never complain about a woefully ill-advised tattoo a guy gets when he's seriously wasted, because she's the one who makes him get it.

5. Bad girls typically wear sexier shoes.

6. If she's a bad girl, that means she has a bunch of bad-girl friends — which also means the guy's friends will buy him drinks all night as long as he introduces them.

7. Yes, the arguments are terrible, but the makeup sex is mind-blowing.

8. Bad girls never ask a guy why he just throws his dirty socks on the floor rather than putting them in the hamper…She's too busy ripping all of his other clothes off.

9. If a guy says, "God, you have an awesome [body part]!" she'll smile and shake said body part, not giggle and cover it up.

10. That fantasy he has that requires handcuffs lots of leather, and a hand puppet? Hell, a bad girl will try anything once.

11. Bad girls can appreciate a good dirty joke... and even better; tell one that's 10 times dirtier.

12. A bad girl is way too independent to rush a relationship, which means a guy knows he won't find himself helping her dad build a model railroad on the third date.

It seems men want their cake and eat it too. Most of the men polled reluctantly agreed they wouldn't want to marry a bad girl just have fun with them. What is a girl to do with that conundrum? Easy, just learn to balance the good with the *BAD!* Know when to turn it on and off. Become a master at this and you can have and keep any man you want!

4

THE PSYCHOLOGY BEHIND MEN AND PROSTITUTES

Charlie Sheen and his addiction to the bad girl. It has been beaten to death. He is the poster boy for all wayward actors gone berserk. Charlie Sheen reportedly ran up a $26,000 prostitute tab one weekend in early January -- good thing he makes $1.8 million per episode of 'Two and a Half Men.' or should I say used to.

The hard-partying star, whose life has swung out of control the past few months after throwing a fit in a restaurant and then trashing a New York hotel room with a prostitute in a closet, has been living in a drug-fueled trance in Las Vegas, and RadarOnline.com now reports that Sheen's latest outburst involved copious amounts of cocaine and paid-for sex.

Fueled by the drug, the site says Sheen paid $10,000 to a prostitute named Ginger for four hours of sex, and earlier, $8,000 to two others. In one day. They met him at his $40,000 a night suite at the Palms Resort, where he continued to take drugs even as he focused on the tasks at hand.

Sheen also hung out with at least three porn stars that weekend (including Best Anal Award winner Bree Olson), and introduced his ex-wife Denise Richards to a prostitute that fateful night in November.

Sheen was arrested in December and spent Christmas in a Colorado jail.

With other cases such as Eliot Spitzer's latest scandal, as well as other male politicians whose prostitution habits had been found out by the general public, many may be asking themselves–What drives these men to fornicate with prostitutes? Is it all men and we just happen to shed light on politicians and point fingers as if men all over the place aren't doing the same thing? What is it about prostitutes, in particular, that drive these men crazy to the point of risking their careers and putting their families on the line?

What must first be understood is the psychological appeal of prostitutes, which is what Michael Bader of AlterNet, a person who has studied the dynamics of sexual arousal for almost 15 years, has spoken out about in order to create a sense of understanding.

When it comes to a regular relationship, it is said that men feel as if they must give a great deal to their partner in order to get a little something back. Our culture represents women as high maintenance individuals who must be cared for by a man and are otherwise helpless in life, always needing the attention and demanding the security of a man. While those exaggerations are often false, it is our society that has conditioned men to believe that this is true, making their intimate relationships suffer when it comes to a man who wishes to have his needs met and they begin to freak out and are said to be overwhelmed by what is expected of them.

It does not matter what *type* of prostitute a man is hiring, it can be a woman who charges over $5,000 for an hour or it can be a woman prostituting herself on the street for $50 a night, what it comes down to is that when payment is made, the man is getting his wishes tended to. It is said that while politicians, in particular, are used to wielding power and keeping people under him in check, no one is working for this man without getting something in return–and that is where the appeal of prostitutes comes in.

A prostitute serves as a slave to a man's needs. She is an actress, although to the man, he does not care that what he is receiving for his money is a one-woman play and an act that he gets to be nothing but a prop in. This is the man's time to shine and get whatever sexual kink he has attended to–No questions asked and no need to reciprocate. A prostitute is sought out when a man wishes to let go and selfishly indulge in his desires without having to give anything back to the woman who performs for him.

So basically, prostitution is sought out when men realize that they cannot handle what is expected of them as men and want to be entirely selfish in their actions even when what society depicts most women to be is false. Prostitutes are wanted by the men who don't want to sexually please their wives or even care about *her* desires, but women can most definitely be counted on to be standing by their selfish, hypocritical and cheating men. Breaking wedding vows never needed many psychological explanations before, so here's the Reader's Digest version:

He does not want to be in a relationship; instead, he wants someone who will make him look like a "family man" who cares about and loves his family so he can get a few votes and make his way into office where even more stress will be put upon him. He wants this while he can also go behind his wife's back and get his needs met while constantly complaining that his wife wants too much from him. My advice is to go out and find a man who can indulge in his kinky desires with you, while you are comfortable enough to know that he will do the same for you. Open and honest communication never hurt a relationship, either…Who knew?

Basic Instinct

Of course, the simplest explanation for men buying sex is that they like it. After all, people are generally willing to pay for activities they enjoy as much as they do sex. On the other hand, a man can usually get sex for free in the context of an ordinary intimate relationship. So why pay good money for it, especially given the social and health risks of having sex with a prostitute? Are all johns so unappealing that they cannot get sex any other way?

Most researchers do not think so. Johns come from all socioeconomic classes, according to culture researcher Sabine Grenz of Humboldt University of Berlin. They may be stockbrokers, truck drivers, teachers, priests or law-enforcement officials. Many are married with children. "There are no social characteristics that basically distinguish johns from other men," says Grenz, who published her interviews with a large number of johns in a 2005 book.

Nor are these men defined by obvious personality problems. In a survey published in 1994 psychologist Dieter Kleiber of the Free University of Berlin had some 600 johns fill out the Freiburg Personality Inventory and found no particular abnormalities. The only correlations he found applied to risk taking and unprotected sex. For example, the men who demanded sex without condoms tended to score higher on aggression and married and well-to-do customers practiced unprotected sex more frequently than others did. "The more secure and orderly a man's life is, the more he believes in his own invulnerability," Kleiber concludes.

5

THE ART OF BECOMING A BAD GIRL

Men are natural aggressors and like to do the hunting. Bad girls tease and flirt but never emasculate the man by being too forward. There is an art to knowing when to turn it on and off. I would recommend reading books about Courtesans as they are the original bad girl seductresses trained in the art of pleasing men.

The Courtesan is Enthusiastically Sexual. The Courtesan understands that men want a sexually enthusiastic woman, not a girl that is a bored in bed and just goes through the motions out of duty. The Courtesan embraces that she's a sexual woman and has no hang-ups about it. When she's alone she regularly fantasizes and is not shy about masturbating herself to orgasm. Whenever she sees her lover she's overcome with fresh enthusiasm and with barely restrained eagerness.

The Courtesan is Uninhibited. The Courtesan delights in being a "bad girl" for her man, and is always willing to go farther. Once she gets an idea, she runs with it. She's passionate, hot, fun, and raw in the bedroom.

The Courtesan is Visual. The Courtesan understands that men want to look and sex is as exciting as what he sees. She makes herself as feminine as possible, dressing so that the most interesting portions of her anatomy are emphasized. She wears sexy costumes and eats right and takes care of her body. She uses visual techniques and nonverbal cues during sex to maximize her man's excitement.

The Courtesan is a Dancer. She moves sexy, abandoning herself in dance. It is the way she dances that makes her man's heart pound, her whole body alive, writhing like an animal in heat. Her dancing may be hardly professional, but she enjoys herself so much and is so unrestrained that none of that matters.

The Courtesan embodies Variety. She is not repetitive. She is versed in a myriad of fantasies and techniques. She makes it a delightful game to play new fantasy roles, to surprise her man, and to be an endless source of entertainment to him. A man grows bored with a woman, no matter how beautiful. He yearns for different pleasures, and for adventure. The Courtesan offers such variety and adventure.

The Courtesan is Devoted to Pleasure. She is the incarnation of all that is exciting and titillating. She knows what pleases and she is devoted to the art of pleasure for both herself and to her lover.

Steps to start taking now:

Steps to becoming irresistible to men

1. So maybe you were raised to be a proper young lady, put restrictions on yourself, or always tried to live to other

people's ideas and standards. Now you want to enhance your life or a relationship that is in a rut and needs a bit of fresh air. Whatever the case, here's a starter list.

2. Make a plan and include an end goal. No matter what anyone has ever said, great achievements haven't been accomplished without some goal in mind and a plan, however loose, to get there. Remember that small goals along the way are key. If you go straight for the big time, chances are you will only fall flat and ruin the desire. My wife didn't go right into five inch stilettos; she started with 3.5 inch... after she almost broke her ankle, knee and shoulder.

3. Commit. Tell yourself you will and stay with it, especially on the bad days.

4. You'll love this part... go shopping! Not being stereotypical, but who doesn't enjoy going out and getting a new set of threads that you know will create a new feeling or enhance older ones? Shopping list is pretty simple and easy for the most part.

5. Panties. Boy shorts, g-strings, thongs, even bikinis will do the trick. The thong/g-string route is not comfortable at first, but becomes better shortly according to my wife and her friends.

6. Bras. Most importantly, get measured to make sure you are about to buy the right size. Go look for shelf bras, push-ups and a corset or bustier. You want to unleash that wild side. These are for special occasions right? Push-ups will certainly bring the *girls* into light, corsets and bustier will add some

sexy playfulness and the shelf bra is going to leave very, VERY, little to the imagination. Yours, hers or his. The first two are easy to fit for. The shelf bra is tricky. The bottom of the breasts are supported and maybe some cleavage or maybe not. The one thing for sure - your nipples are not covered. That is the temptress part!!! Be wary of any shelf that contains boning unless you have implants. Just doesn't do you any justice nor will it achieve the effect desired visually or mentally.

7. Stockings. You are most likely not going to find the sexy stuff unless you go to a specialty store or shop online. Thigh highs, seamed back, crotch less, fence net, lace, fishnet, the list goes on and on.

8. Shoes. Boots or high heels... or both! You are faced with some simple issues here actually. Mental comfort. You can't worry what others think, especially strangers. But, you still have to have the mental assurance. If you don't feel like you are sexy walking in some spiked heels, you won't be. Look for height, style and comfort in that order. Height is for you and you alone to determine. The style is where is gets complicated. Some things are classic such as black high heels or knee high boots. Buy something abnormal. Thigh high boots and over-the-knee boots are actually gaining acceptance. Don't rule either out. But don't go overboard unless you are really sure.

9. All those things you have accepted as being slutty or whorish or that make your preacher blush... that's what you want on naughty occasions. To some extent anyway. Go

ahead and wear that skirt that is two to four inches too short, or that see-through shirt, and get a bit brighter and daring with the make-up and hair. Start the evening or day with intent!

10. There are two types of naughty. Work and Date.

11. Work. This obviously isn't the place to sport the Julia Roberts in Pretty Woman hooker boots. Probably not where you want to wear the heavy make-up or see-through blouse. What's a girl to do? Bring your panties, in your purse. That shelf bra would make a perfect wear-under-a-loose-shirt here. Wear those crotch less panties or stockings. That lipstick that requires batteries is an excellent choice to take the bathroom with you on short break. Only you know what is going on in all of these circumstances so it makes it all daring and stimulating. Kind of feels rebellious or may even make for some titillating conversation amongst the ladies.

12. Dates. Yes married people still need to *date* if you will. You need to go out and treat each other to a nice event. Of course all of the cliché tips come in here. Go take your panties off in the bathroom, put them in his pocket, play footsy with his crotch, blah blah blah. How about really changing it up. Make sure he knows beforehand that you aren't wearing panties; then, seductively remind him every so often. Nothing says "I am teasing you" like his asking the waiter for a dirty martini and your softly whispering something like your "uncovered nether region is feeling dirty right now."

13. Now is where the shelf or no-cup bra really comes into play. A thin shirt on top of it allows you to rub against him or poke him at will and drive him CRAZY! Play a game of no touch. Basically, you can touch all you want, but he cannot!

14. When you are getting dressed, if you are wearing a button-up blouse, look at where you normally leave it unbuttoned to. Then open one or two more. It will take a bit to get used to, but only a couple of hours.

15. If you decide to wear those crotch less panties or go without, sit beside him on the inside of the booth or closest to the wall if you are at a table. If your table is out in the open area of the floor just make sure you pull the table cloth over your lap. Hold his hand that is closest to you, then randomly run it up your skirt or high on your pants leg just long enough to ensure he gets the idea and feeling, but not so long that it attracts attention from others. Unless that is your thing.

16. Going for the old take 'em off in the bathroom trick?! Use the same tip above or really surprise him. Drop your napkin or something really close to your feet and then ask him to pick it up. When he leans over, make sure he gets a good view.

17. Other nice to haves or to-do's. There is always something that can be used or done to spice it up. If you have the opportunity, then take it. Have the kids planned for a sleep-over at someone's house? Then meet him at the door in nothing more than a smile and an apron. Try just wearing one of his ties. Check the peep hole before you try this trick for

sure. Nothing says welcome like greeting the pizza delivery dude buck naked. (You may get free pizza!) Not sure when the kids are due in... pull him straight from the front door to the bedroom. Mental scars are difficult to heal. Yours or theirs. What about a leather bra, feather boa or something else along those lines.

Tips

* Search online for anything you are looking for. Several of the open cup bras, different style panty hose and other lingerie pieces are available at deep discounts at places such as Amazon.com.

* Look for something scary and that's probably what you want. If your stomach turns or you get a bad feeling, then that is too far. Attitude is 95% of sexy and it will show if you aren't comfortable.

* When ordering high heels, get a good measurement to start from. Then add a 1/2 size for 3-4 inch heels, 1 full size for 5-6 inches, 1.5 or 2 sizes for 7 and 8 inch heels. Reality says much past 4 inches will not work to your favor as comfort in any sense will fail you. The really extreme heels are best for the bedroom!

* Don't forget to check out the return policy!!!

* Don't be scared to return something. Most underwear items

are prohibited from returns by Fed Laws. Keep that in mind when buying panties or stockings.

* Look over his shoulder, browse the web or pick around to get ideas to begin with if need be. Talk with other women.

* Trips to vacation spots or far away towns where no one knows you are the easiest places try the new styles.

Warnings

* Keep the local laws in mind.

* If you are talking it over with your girlfriend or another woman, keep it more of a "what do you do" conversation and not an "I'm broke, please help me get fixed" style. It only opens the door for underhanded comments or other thing of that nature, plus it's really between you and your lover!

* Ensure you know the company dress code or informal policies before you strut it up in the workplace.

* Never chance letting a minor see, when you are turning the heat up. Many parents overreact and the entire evening will be spoiled.

* If you can't do it with a smile on the inside, don't do it at all. Hurting yourself just to please someone else is not worth it in the long run. You will grow contempt and frustration towards that person.

6

BAD GIRL SEX TRICKS

According to an article in Cosmopolitan by Benjamin; Bad girls are legendary — a guy who's been with one practically passes out from bliss when he talks about his experience. You might be thinking, "Who, me? Be a bad girl?" But any woman who wants to can wake up her hibernating vixen...and have a damn good time doing it!

See, bed-devil status is about a fearless attitude, not how much sexual experience you have or whether you wear leather. "Guys dig when women are unbridled and uninhibited, push their own boundaries, break the rules, and ask for what they want," says Barbara Keesling, PhD, author of *The Good Girl's Guide to Bad Girl Sex*. So we boiled down the naughty qualities that make some women stand out, then came up with seven audacious ideas for putting them into play. These tips and tricks will forever crank up the heat in your sex life.

DARE: Be the Boss in Bed Tonight

A wickedly sexy woman knows how to deliciously exploit the power she has over a man. Tell your guy to lie down on the bed, then use handcuffs, scarves, or a necktie to tether his hands together so he can't touch you. (If you're not game to use real restraints, you can simply hold his hands over his head.)

Next, "you want to torture him playfully with your teasing," says sex expert Candida Royalle, author of *How to Tell a Naked Man What to Do*. "Slowly kiss your way down his torso, and just as you get to his pelvis, move back up to his ears and neck."

As you tantalize him and he strains to touch you, ask him to tell you why he wants you so bad, explaining that you won't let him free until he convinces you. Once he's pleaded his case, release his hands, roll onto your back, and allow him to take over. After building up the erotic anticipation, it'll be like setting a windup toy loose on your body...and hearing him describe how hot you are will turbo charge your experience too.

DARE: Slip into a Naughty Costume

To infuse your sex sessions with more attitude, sometimes all it takes is looking the part of a true temptress. "One of the ways a woman can really show off her sexuality is by playing up different sides of her erotic personality," explains Jamye Waxman, author of *Getting Off*.

If you're feeling like a flirty, girlie tease, put on white cotton undie set or pale pink lingerie and pull your hair into a ponytail, or don a schoolgirl-like plaid miniskirt with an oxford shirt tied above your navel. To become an X-rated seductress, wear something red or black in sheer fabric or lace, and then add crimson lipstick and nails. "Outfits not only help you get in the moment, they also give him a visual turn-on and inspiration," adds Waxman.

Just standing there in your flimsy finest may be enough, but a few teasing lines will definitely get the ball rolling. When playing the innocent card, say it's your first time, and ask him what you should do. As a seductress, whisper all the different ways and places you want to touch him.

DARE: Learn to Talk Dirty

Moans and sighs (*Oh! Oh!*) are easy. It's the dirty dialogue that really puts a triple-X stamp on your sex sessions. "Talking dirty heightens the whole experience, keeps you both present, and turns you on even more," says Royalle. "Plus, men actually like being told what to do in bed because it helps them get it right."

First tell him how freakin' good he feels. (Tongue-tied? Try no-fail lines like "You feel so/You make me [adjective]"; "I love it when you [verb] my [body part].") Then you're set to show him the way to send you soaring, with something like, "*Oooh*, almost there. I need your [noun] on my [body part], just like this."

DARE: Watch Yourselves Having Sex

Body confidence and carnal curiosity are key traits of a sex goddess, and both are on full display when you make a sex tape. "Seeing yourselves midact gives you a voyeuristic thrill, almost as though you're peeping into your own bedroom. It feels taboo," explains Royalle. "You also get to see how your partner is responding and how you look when you're getting off." If you're worried about becoming the next Kim Kardashian, skip the tape and just hook the video camera directly up to a television in your bedroom — without recording — and watch yourselves *while* you're going at it.

Since missionary doesn't exactly make for good TV, get into racier positions where you're facing the camera. Go for doggie-style so you can both see the action or girl-on-top so you can watch exactly how you move. And definitely get shots exchanging oral sex so you can see the orgasmic effect you have on each other.

DARE: Summon His Buried Bad Boy

Bad girls are known to capture a few prisoners in the sack, but a bold bedroom chick also enjoys enacting her own fantasies, shame-free. And one of women's top fantasies is to be taken. "It's a turn-on to feel like he wants you so bad, he just can't help himself, explains Keesling. "Plus, when he's being aggressive, you have to fully give up the reins, which can help you be even more in the here and now."

Instruct your guy to hide behind the door and "surprise" you by taking charge when you get home one night. He can either have his way with you right in the foyer or pull you into the bedroom. Or let him know that you're in the mood but want him to conquer you, caveman-style, even if it means playfully wrestling you to the bed as you try to slip out of his grasp.

DARE: Give Him a Jolt

Breaking out of your touch-here-then-lick-there routine adds a lusty layer to the erotic experience. And fearless sexual playmates know that unexpectedly intense sexual maneuvers are even more exciting. "A forceful touch snaps your guy into the moment and heightens every sensation that follows, "says Royalle. "The spontaneity also keeps him anticipating each touch, magnifying his excitement." Plus, the implied roughness invites him to tap in to his primal, wild sexual self.

Grip his butt hard while in missionary, scratch his chest and the sides of his torso while in girl-on-top, or yank his head toward you to give him a passionate, damn-straight kind of kiss. If those moves elicit an excited response, firmly spank his butt, lightly bite his shoulder, or tug his hair in the act, you devilish thing.

DARE: Try Some Naughty Props

Do something unexpected with toys you already have lying around the house.

Hairbrush: A hard-bristled hairbrush is perfect for gently scratching his skin.

Rolling pin: Run this baker's basic over his back and thighs during an erotic massage.

Blush brush: Skip the pricey feathers you find at sex shops, and use this to tickle his neck, chest, arms, and package.

Becoming a Bad Girl in the work place

Rules in the workplace are completely different than with attracting men. According to an article by

Laurel Delaney Bad girls finish first in business!

Rules for the Worldly Woman Warrior in All of Us

Want to become one of the most powerful and influential global businesswomen on the planet? I do! Then dismount your Harley and start working on it. But first, you have to learn how to become a bad girl, because bad girls always finish first.

Break a Rule, Bad Girl

How do bad girls finish first? They act free, take on challenges, break rules. If you don't, it's over. Constantly learn and change, be persuasive, dare to be different, have extraordinary stamina and never stop imagining possibilities. The bad girl mantra is "if you can imagine it, you can do it."

Bad girls also know how to create teams of diverse people who are very loyal, yet also challenge and push their leader to achieve. And, they make sure that everyone remembers them as a bad girl because they don't care about being a good girl. Bad girls finish first.

Tying the Knot, but not Around Your Neck

Do good girls think marriage moves them along in their career? Will having an ordinary, less than supportive spouse take away from their drive and initiative? Do they think that having children will bring out their softer, more sensitive side to being a businesswoman? Or will that be cause for tossing their desire to the wind?

From my own personal and professional lifestyle choices to those of top businesswoman Carly Fiorina, CEO of H-P, there will always be some good girl lurking in the background criticizing us. Yet, the name of the game is to just live your life. Since Carly is a better bad girl than I am and more well known, let's zero in on her talents for a moment.

Grit, Guts and Luck

She has accomplished great things in the business world; but when women size her up, they say she had this uncanny good fortune of working for one of the few in America who made promoting women a top priority. Coincidentally, Carly also married a man who took early retirement and happened to have two children from a previous marriage. Many viewed this as a happy 'instant' family for Carly when, in fact, she most likely fell in love with a man and took on the responsibility of nurturing a healthy relationship with his kids as well. Fortunately, with her smarts and ambition, she chose the right man and the right job for herself. Luck, guts, persistence and good timing made her life choices work for her in all respects. She chose to be a bad girl. Bad girls finish first.

It's Not a Glass Ceiling -- It's a Guy block in Disguise

Remember the saying, "Ginger Rogers did everything Fred Astaire did, but backwards." Well, that's us, bad girls! Now we just rev up our Harleys. The good girls let the guys lead.

The bad girls don't. They size up guys from head to just below the waist. They're an aggressive group that knows how to bust through a guy block in disguise.

What's to fear? You can see through a glass ceiling, but not a guy block. It's rock solid and it holds you back, but not for long. Take your well-deserved seat in the executive suite. Let's show them what we're made of. Aim for results, nothing less. Fear lies in the eyes of the beholder, and that beholder becomes the guy block. Let's tackle and break their force. Go ahead, make their day. Good girls glaze at glass ceilings and forever wonder while bad girls tackle guy blocks. Be a bad girl.

Ambition -- Push Hard to Get to the Top

I consider ambition to be something you can't live without. Like oxygen, it's something you need. To adjust your ambition to someone else's lower level is to prepare yourself for death. Bad girls refuse to decrease their ambition, for it is a part of who they are.

Many times after completing an "ambitious" project, I have been asked, "Who told you that you could do that?" My response is "me." It's considered extremely ambitious, by good girls' standards, to take your life into your own hands and just do what you feel like doing without worrying about what people will say or think. I find it liberating to do this, and I hope you will too. Compelling ambition is when you decide to do what you want to do, regardless of support or knowing in advance the outcome. Push hard. Don't take "no" for an answer. Be aggressive. Drive hard. Forget about what people think. It's what YOU think that matters. Don't let other people's mediocre expectations of you become the truth about your life.

You good girls out there, who have self-doubts and poor self-esteem, listen up! The bad girls are going to help you. Bad girls know that ambition is about unlocking, unbottling and unleashing your energy to reach your full potential. Bad girls know how to make their mark. They maintain clarity and initiative and don't care about appearing combative -- they just do their jobs. You want to be a good girl? Fine, then you're not going to get ahead, because bad girls always finish first.

Unabashed Immodesty -- Taking Center Stage

While doing a good job, good girls are scaredy-cats -- they are afraid to toot their own horns. What will people think? They never want to be improper or appear unladylike. God help them. Bad girls are energetic tigers -- they network like crazy, get jobs done and let the whole world know about it. Get over your immodesty and shyness and proclaim your strengths with a sense of fury and fire. Call attention to your accomplishments, intelligence and emotions! Work hard at gaining recognition for your abilities! If you don't, who will? Be a bad girl.

Inner Strength and the Power of Optimism

A dear friend of mine dated a man she was crazy about for five years. She confessed to me that she shared her secrets and her soul with him. She had trusted beyond belief. When it came time for the big one -- commitment -- he looked the other way. Why? Because that day, he didn't like the weather. My reaction? I thought it was a wonderful stroke of luck for her. Had he made the commitment she thought she was ready for, she would have gone off into the sunset with him and settled for someone who was nowhere near her equal. This strength and ability to pull on optimism in what seemed like a very dark moment carried her through to the point of looking at new possibilities in a whole new light. A light that shined a bright new future on her.

The whole incident became a meaningful signal to redirect her life. And she did. Sometimes, not getting what you want can make you fearless in getting what you need. Furthermore, a disaster that blindsides us typically provides a moment to rid ourselves of all our mistakes and begin anew. Don't let emotions cloud your judgment. It's clear this friend of mine is not one of the good girls. With optimism like this, she will pull ahead. She's a bad girl.

To Compromise or Not to Compromise?

Make a shameful or disreputable concession? Awe, come now, do you want to remain a good girl? Go ahead. Us bad girls will ride our Harleys full-throttle and leave you in the dust, because a concession is the same as a compromise. And with too many compromises, you lose focus.

In the line of fire, never compromise. Good girls compromise. Bad girls don't. So you wanna be a 'sexy' brain surgeon? Get started. Stick to your guns. Know what you want. Have a clear mental picture of your target. Then fire. Eliminate the getting ready and aiming part. That's tedious. Besides, who has the time? If you miss your target, fire again. The point is to just keep firing until you get what you want. Stay on course with your conviction and vision. It's so very simple, you boring good girls. Why can't you listen to us bad girls?

And, for all you bad girls, if you absolutely must compromise -- go ahead -- but remember who's in charge: YOU. Don't sacrifice your soul, for your soul carries you through to your destiny. Did you get that? Soul. Pure. Simple. Lock it up. Throw away the key. It's yours, and only yours, for keeps.

Don't Sit on the Sidelines -- Feel Good About Yourself and Get Out There

How can you possibly conquer the world if you don't feel good about yourself? Overcome the urge to sit back on the sidelines and be a good-girl, just observing because you're afraid to say what's on your mind. Don't worry about saying the wrong thing. What's a wrong thing? And, who said so? Do you care?

Also, be willing to fail. Know it's a possibility. Look it in the eye. Conquer it. And then, move on. In the process, figure yourself out because that is your single greatest gift and most powerful lifeforce. Grow or get lost. And if you should decide to drop out or disappear, even for a moment, there's no chance you will ever become a true leader. Fight with all your might to be and promote your real self. Exude confidence and dare to be different. Always. Constantly. No variance. Be a bad girl.

Relishing Risk

One good girl's timidity is another bad girl's big win, but that victory will not come unless a calculated risk is involved. True risk -- that sudden leap into the unknown -- can carry you into a state of nirvana. Do what's unconventional, disconcerting or unexpected. Take a chance. Take a risk. And keep taking them -- that's how you learn, grow, rediscover and develop. Bad girls who are creative, innovative, transformative, experimental and visionary absolutely take risks in order to earn their much-deserved rewards. Strive everyday to do OOT -- one outrageous thing. If you feel perspiration beading high on your forehead, then you know you're onto OOT. Be eager to test what works. The whole point is to take yourself in a new direction and succeed.

Thrive [or Die], You Bad Girl!

Create your own opportunities. Explore and make your deepest BIG dreams become a reality. Even if you lack support, embrace who you are. Own, honor, utilize and validate your innate gifts. Pay attention to your integrity and go out there and unfold your destiny that flows from character and live a life filled with surprises. Move fast. Have the fury of the wind behind you. Create a sense of urgency. Use your gifts to achieve success. Soar to greatness. Set yourself up to survive at an optimum level in your life and enjoy your exciting and rewarding journey to mastering your own life. Be a bad girl.

7

BAD GIRL RULES

1) Beauty is Pain

There is no such thing as natural beauty, only a good canvas to start off with. Beauty involves exercise, waxing, tweezers, and in some cases cosmetic surgery (ugly or fat girls) or Botox needles (older women). But no matter how good or bad a canvas, beauty is within your reach...if you have the pain threshold for it.

2) Nails are Painted

Fake nails are unacceptable and hoe-ish. Your toes and hands should always be filed, painted and matching. Most colors are accepted. However they should be confined to shades of pink, red, blue, and other dark hues. Never black.

3) Love is a Fairy Tale

There is no such thing as love, it was invented by Disney. A true bad girl never falls in love, for love will is ruins. The truly gifted however can use the idea of "love" to their advantage…

4) Boys are Toys

All men are the same, equally worthless. They are toys that we play with and manipulate for our pleasure. A true bad girl knows this and only uses men for money, muscle (a goon on your side is always helpful) and occasionally sex.

5) Sex is a Weapon

Sex is a bad girl's secret weapon and only a select few should ever experience that treasure. Sex is always a question and will always be answered by the one how holds the power, the women. If anyone doubts that, you introduce them to your gun (guns are for girls). We withhold sex and we give it always to our advantage. Also, we never appreciate.

6) If you got it flaunt it

If you have the body, flaunt it but never expose full nudity. A bad girl must uphold higher standards.

7) Every bad deserves a good licking

The final bad girl rule may be the most important. A bad girl always is smooth down under. And the only way to assure smoothness is the Brazilian wax.

8) Carry your own condoms

According to the Centers for Disease Control and Prevention, the top 10 killers of Americans are heart disease, cancer, stroke, chronic lower respiratory diseases, accidents, Alzheimer's disease, diabetes, influenza and pneumonia, nephritis and septicemia. That sexually transmitted disease that we all fear didn't make the top 10. So throw out your cigarettes and stop eating greasy burgers every day.

However, that doesn't mean you shouldn't be concerned about STDs or pregnancy. Your responsibility as a "bad girl" is to protect yourself and the person you're with. Don't expect him to carry a condom. That's your job. Keep some in your purse at all times.

9) Don't get drunk and then have sex

If you're about to have a one night stand, do it sober. Why? You'll probably not bother with a condom if you're drunk. When you wake up in the morning, you'll know who you slept with. If you decide, last minute, you don't want to sleep with him because he's creepy; it's easier to get away from him if you're not loaded.

There's more, but you get the gist.

10) Don't wait by the phone after sex

You met him; you had sex and now you can't stop thinking about him. But there's been no calls, no texts and you're getting a little pissed.

Did you forget? You're a proud "bad girl." He'll call you when he wants another booty call, if he wants another booty call. Snap out of it and move on.

11) Keep your business to yourself

If you confess to your girlfriends that you slept with yet another man, some of them may feel sorry for you and nag you to change. Again, many people are of the belief that a woman who sleeps around does it because she can't get a man to love her. If you subject yourself to that you'll start believing it. In addition, don't confess your actions to the parents. Chances are they won't understand why their darling daughter is sleeping with so many men.

12) Don't sleep with her husband, your girlfriend's ex-boyfriend or your boss

He has a cute face, a cute butt, and he's been flirting with you for quite some time. He'd love to get with you. Except for one problem, he's married. Let him fool around with someone else. Don't you be the one.

Same goes for your girlfriend's ex. She may say she doesn't care, but she does.

Sleeping with your boss isn't a good idea, either. When you break his heart, you may lose that coveted job.

There's plenty of fish in the sea. Choose one that's not on a hook.

8

BAD GIRL SONGS

Pull out your IPods girls and load up this highly motivational Bad Girl playlist. These songs will kick start your bad girl lessons. So turn them up and enjoy being wicked!

Bad Girl - 1993 - Madonna

Bad Girlfriend – 2008 – Theory Of A Deadman

Rhiannon - Stevie Nicks

Maneater - Hall and Oats

Roxanne - Sting

Black magic woman - Santana

Witchy woman - Eagles

These boots are made for walking' - Nancy Sinatra

Call me - Deborah Harry

Dark Lady - Cher

Long Cool Woman in a Black Dress - The Hollies

Green Eyed Lady - Sugarloaf

Alligator Woman - Cameo

Devil Woman - Cliff Richard

Mustang Sally - Wilson Pickett

Devil in Her Heart - The Beatles

Runaround Sue - Dion

Wicked Game - Chris Isaak

You ought a know - Alannis Morisette

So What - Pink

Killer Queen - Queen

Animal - Neon Trees

Bad Medicine - Bon Jovi

Cold As Ice - Foreigner

Dangerous - Kardinal Offishall

Dangerous - Roxette

Dangerous - James Blunt

Dirty Diana - Michael Jackson

Dixie Chicken - Little Feat

Evil Woman - Electric Light Orchestra

Girl - The View

Hell on the Heart - Eric Church

Highly Strung - Spandau Ballet

Hooray for Hazel - Tommy Roe

Keeps Gettin' Better - Christina Aguilera

Le Disko - Shiny Toy Guns

Maneater - Nelly Furtado

Modern Day Delilah - Kiss

Poison - Bell Biv DeVoe

Poison Ivy - The Coasters

Poison Ivy - The Jonas Brothers

Serpentine - Disturbed

The Girl Who Destroys - Amber Pacific

Tokyo Rose - Idle Eyes

Turn So Cold - Drowning Pool

Won't Go Quietly - Example

Words - The Monkees

You Give Love A Bad Name - Bon Jovi

You Got Me - Crash Kings

Your Time Is Gonna Come - Led Zeppelin

Classic Bad Girl song Lyrics

Donna Summer - Bad Girl Lyrics

Toot toot hey beep beep

Bad girls
talking about the sad girls
sad girls
talking about the bad girls, yeah

See them out on the street at night, walkin'
picking up on all kinds of strangers
if the price is right you can score
if you're pocket's nice
but you want a good time
you ask yourself, who they are?
like everybody else, they come from near and far

Bad girls
talking about the sad girls
sad girls
talking about the bad girls, yeah

Friday night and the strip is hot
sun's gone down and they're about to trot
spirit's high and they look hot

do you wanna get down
now don't you ask yourself, who they are?
like everybody else, they wanna be a star

Sad girls, sad girls
you such a dirty bad girl
beep beep uh, uh
you bad girl, you sad girl
you such a dirty bad girl
beep beep uh, uh

Now you and me, we are both the same
but you call yourself by different names
now you mama won't like it when she finds out
her girl is out at night

Toot toot hey beep beep

Hey mister, have you got a dime?
mister, do you want to spend some time, oh yeah
I got what you want
you got what I need
I'll be your baby
come and spend it on me
hey mister
I'll spend some time with you
with you, you're fine, with you
bad girls
they're just bad girls
talkin' about sad girls
sad girls
hey, hey mister
got a dime?

Toot toot hey beep

"Witchy Woman" - Eagles

Raven hair and ruby lips
sparks fly from her finger tips
Echoed voices in the night
she's a restless spirit on an endless flight
wooo hooo witchy woman, see how
high she flies
woo hoo witchy woman she got
the moon in her eye
She held me spellbound in the night
dancing shadows and firelight
crazy laughter in another
room and she drove herself to madness
with a silver spoon
woo hoo witchy woman see how high she flies
woo hoo witchy woman she got the moon in her eye
Well I know you want a lover,
let me tell your brother, she's been sleeping
in the Devil's bed.
And there's some rumors going round
someone's underground
she can rock you in the nighttime
'til your skin turns red
woo hoo witchy woman
see how high she flies
woo hoo witchy woman
she got the moon in her eye

Rhiannon - Stevie Nicks

Rhiannon rings like a bell through the night and
Wouldn't you love to love her?

Takes to the sky like a bird in flight and
Who will be her lover?

All your life you've never seen
A woman taken by the wind
Would you stay if she promised you heaven?
Will you ever win?

She is like a cat in the dark and then
She is the darkness
She rules her life like a fine skylark and when
The sky is starless

All your life you've never seen
A woman taken by the wind
Would you stay if she promised you heaven?
Will you ever win?
Will you ever win?

Rhiannon
Rhiannon
Rhiannon
Rhiannon

She rings like a bell through the night and
Wouldn't you love to love her?
She rules her life like a bird in flight and
Who will be her lover?

All your life you've never seen
A woman taken by the wind
Would you stay if she promised you heaven?
Will you ever win?
Will you ever win?

Rhiannon

Rhiannon
Rhiannon

Taken by
Taken by the sky

Taken by
Taken by the sky

Taken by
Taken by the sky

Dreams unwind
Loves a state of mind

Dreams unwind
Loves a state of mind

Dreams unwind
Loves a state of mind...

Britney Spears featuring Lil Wayne - Bad Girl Lyrics

If you want it
Come and get it
Yeah

1,7 eagle, eagle
Weezy my name
Yup
… fire fire
Till no more flame left
We da people who ya people told you not to speak to
Peepz will leave you sleepin with the people right beneath you

I would like to ignite this track with my ..
I would fight like 20 rounds
I gotta do Wayne
Weezy F baby, baby I keep my shoes clean
Shirt always matchin, stay in my new jeans

…………..

I've been a bad girl …
I must admit this
Welcome to my world in case you missed it
I'm a big deal, its kinda twisted
But let's just keep it real, I'm the hottest misfit

(If you want it, come and get it)

I'm a bad girl I'ma do what I do
I can have my cake and eat it too
A girl like me will bring you to your knees
'Cause that's what bad girls do

I'm a bad girl I'ma do what I do
I can have my cake and eat it too
A girl like me will bring you to your knees
'Cause that's what bad girls do

Imma bad girl, Imma, Imma bad girl
(I like a bad girl, I like a bad girl)
Imma bad girl, Imma, Imma bad girl
(I like a bad girl, I like a bad girl)

Come and punish me
You can tie me up boy
Do as you please
Make me like I'm your toy
www.musicloversgroup.com

I'm the M.V.P
Can't nobody touch me
This is my ..
You can watch as I ..

(If you want it, come and get it)

I'm a bad girl I'ma do what I do
I can have my cake and eat it too
A girl like me will bring you to your knees
'Cause that's what bad girls do

I'm a bad girl I'ma do what I do
I can have my cake and eat it too
A girl like me will bring you to your knees
'Cause that's what bad girls do

Imma bad girl, Imma, Imma bad girl
(I like a bad girl, I like a bad girl)
Imma bad girl, Imma, Imma bad girl
(I like a bad girl, I like a bad girl)

Bring ya to ya knee's
Bring ya, bring ya to ya knee's
To ya knee's
Bring ya, bring ya, bring ya to ya knee's
Bring ya to ya knee's
Bring ya, bring ya to ya knee's
To ya knee's
Bring ya, bring ya, bring ya to ya knee's

I'm a bad girl I'ma do what I do
I can have my cake and eat it too
A girl like me will bring you to your knees
'Cause that's what bad girls do

I'm a bad girl I'ma do what I do
I can have my cake and eat it too
A girl like me will bring you to your knees
'Cause that's what bad girls do

Imma bad girl, Imma, Imma bad girl
(I like a bad girl, I like a bad girl)
Imma bad girl, Imma, Imma bad girl
(I like a bad girl, I like a bad girl)

Rhiana - "GOOD GIRLS GONE BAD" song lyrics

We stay, moving around, so low
Ask us where you at, we don't know
And don't care (don't care)
All we know is we was at home 'cause you left us there
You got your boys and got gone
And left us all alone

Now she in the club with a freaky dress on
Cats don't wan her to keep that dress on
Trying to get enough drinks in her system
Take it to the telly and make her a victim

Patron in the brain, ball playa in the face
They shake the spot, she's just another case

[chorus]

Easy for a good girl to go bad
And once we gone (Gone)
Best belief we've gone forever
Don't be the reason
Don't be the reason
You better learn how to treat us right
'Cause once a good girl goes bad
We done forever

He's staying with a flock of them all, yeah
Got a girl at home but he don't care
Won't care (Won't care)
All he'll do is keep me at home, won't let me go nowhere
He thinks because I'm at home I won't be getting it on
Now I'm finding numbers in the jacket pockets
Chicks calling the house, no stop it's
Getting out of control
Finally I can't take no more

He finds a letter on the stairs, saying this is the end
I packed my bag and left with your best friend

[chorus]
Easy for a good girl to go bad
And once we gone (Gone)
Best belief we've gone forever
Don't be the reason
Don't be the reason
You better learn how to treat us right
'Cause once a good girl goes bad
We done forever

We stay, moving around, so low
Ask us where you at, we don't know
And don't care (don't care)
All we know is we was at home cause you left us there

You got your boys and got gone
And left us all alone (no)

[chorus]
Easy for a good girl to go bad
And once we gone (Gone)
Best belief we've gone forever
Don't be the reason
Don't be the reason
You better learn how to treat us right
'Cause once a good girl goes bad
We done forever
We gone forever
We gone forever

"Bad Girl"
(feat. Missy Elliott)

When the red light comes on I transform
When the red light comes on I transform

[Aubrey]
Look in my eyes covered in Maybelline
Looking like something fresh out a magazine
I can be part of your deepest fantasies
You're the detective, come solve my mystery

[D. Woods]
Some say that love is all that I'm missing
Some call it jezebel, I call it attention
But what they don't know they can't even imagine
Say I don't have no self-esteem but it's my fashion

[Chorus]

Maybe I'm just a bad girl
Maybe I'm just a bad girl
Maybe I'm just a bad girl
Maybe I'm just a bad girl, a bad girl

I can be your addiction if you wanna get hooked on me
I-I can be your addiction if you wanna get hooked on me

Maybe I'm just a bad girl
Maybe I'm just a bad girl
Maybe I'm just a bad girl
Maybe I'm just a bad girl, a bad girl

When the red light comes on I transform
When the red light comes on I transform
When the red light comes on I transform

[Dawn]
Something about me has got you hypnotized
Examine my body like you're the science guy
Watching my every move you anticipate
What ya thinking about, boy I can recreate

[Aundrea]
Some say that love is all that I'm missing
Some call it jezebel, I call it attention
But what they don't know they can't even imagine
Say I don't have no self-esteem but it's my fashion

[Chorus]

Maybe I'm just a bad girl
Maybe I'm just a bad girl
Maybe I'm just a bad girl
Maybe I'm just a bad girl, a bad girl

[Missy Elliott]
I know you hear me boy...
B-A-D-C-H-I-C, lookin' so sexy
Make them bitches hate me
She not me cause there's just one me
I'm the M to the I-double S-Y-E
Lights come on, I tr-transform
Gimme that dick, baby, com-come on
I can do it all night 'til the break of dawn
On-On and on, I keep on goin'
They call me a jezebel cause I freaks, I does it well
Got extensions in my hair, bad girls is ya'll up in here?
(Yeah)
Tonight we just gonna let it do what it do
I can put this pretty young thing on you
I ain't lookin' for attention, I just want you
Let me be your addiction, I can be that too

I can be your addiction if you wanna get hooked on me
I-I can be your addiction if you wanna get hooked on me

[Chorus]

Maybe I'm just a bad girl
Maybe I'm just a bad girl
Maybe I'm just a bad girl
Maybe I'm just a bad girl, a bad girl

When the red light comes on I transform
When the red light comes on I transform
When the red light comes on I transform

[Shannon + Dawn]
From a caterpillar to a butterfly
I know I got something that you're gonna like
(Don't be afraid I won't let you down)
I'm the one that'll make you come around

[Chorus]

Maybe I'm just a bad girl
Maybe I'm just a bad girl
Maybe I'm just a bad girl
Maybe I'm just a bad girl, a bad girl

9

THE DIFFERENCE BETWEEN BAD AND WRONG

There is a huge difference between bad and wrong. Use your common sense and instincts to help in the balancing act of *Bad* and wrong.

When you have an abundant mentality, you're looking for what is right versus what is wrong.
And we all know those types of people – we may know them personally or intimately (meaning ourselves) – who go into a situation where there could be ten things that are really great, and maybe one thing that is bad or something you don't want. And that one "bad" thing is exactly what you focus on. That's why I wrote the book Perfect Pictures as my very first book. It's about how we're totally focused on trying to create what's perfect. In order to do that, we look for the thing that's wrong, we focus on that, and we try to change it to make everything "perfect."

Again, with the Law of Attraction, what you focus on expands. So even if you notice all these great things in your life, but then you notice this one bad thing and you start focusing on it, you're going to literally shift your vibration from abundance to lack.

So it's important to watch and know – are you a person that is focused on what's right or what's wrong with any given situation? Are you in a relationship? You could be in a relationship with a really great guy or woman – are you focused on all the great qualities about this person? Or are you focused on the fact that he or she didn't do the dishes? Or that he/she didn't give you a compliment? Or that he/she didn't do whatever it was?

So it's really all about where you are focused. That's number one.

The second thing is that there are two sides of every subject. So there is enough, and on the other side, there is not enough. This is a big one. So again, are you focused on the things that are abundant in your life and that you have enough of, or are you focused on the lack of them?

Abundance accounts for everything: love, time, money, whatever. Are you focused on the fact that you don't have enough money or are you focused on the fact that you have enough right now?

Are you focused on the fact that there just isn't enough time? Or are you focused on the fact that you do have enough time, but maybe you just need to organize yourself better? It's really the perception and the way you look at things and the way your mind automatically starts thinking. Most of us are brought up from our parents, socialization, etc…you know, that whole environment with the lack mentality.

And so, when you can really start catching yourself shifting from these lacks to thoughts of abundance – what is right and that there IS enough, then you're going to totally see a different shift in your outer reality.

The next one is a big one for most people. I will say, one hundred percent or at least 9 out of 10 people, when I privately coach them, their biggest issue is getting to that space of "I am enough."

And that is the space of abundance – that "I am enough." And the lack part of it is "I am not enough."

So when you come from a place of "I am not enough," who you are is not enough. You are not thin enough, you are not rich enough, you are not good enough, you are not "whatever it is" enough; you're coming from a lack mentality.

And the most important relationship – the most important point of focus that you have – is the relationship with yourself. And if you can get that right, and start feeling that who you are is enough, and then your whole entire world is going to flip completely upside down.

Now, I will tell you that this is not something that is going to happen overnight. It's not like you are just going to think now that "I am enough" and everything changes. This is something that you will probably have to work on, and retrain within yourself, on a daily basis.
One thing I do want to mention about this is that you are all on a spiritual path, which means that you are on a spiral path – nothing in this life is linear. You don't go from point A to point B and maybe have an issue about not being enough, and kind of work on that issue and go, "Okay, now that's done."

You literally are on a spiral path that moves upwards. What I mean by that is: imagine that you are walking up a spiral staircase, and as you are going up, you may hit a certain point on that path, such as "I'm not enough." And as you go up, you're hitting it again, but you're hitting it from a more elevated place. You're hitting it from a place where you now have different tools and processes to deal with it.

Maybe you feel bad on some level within you, but now you're feeling it at a deeper level. So even though you've hit that before, "I've already felt that and now I'm enough," and then you hit it again, it's not for you to beat yourself up and say, "God, I thought I already did this, and now I'm back at square one?"

It's a matter of knowing that you're just hitting it at a different level; you're hitting it at a deeper level. And you're hitting it from a different place now that you're more abundant. Now that you're being programmed and trained to be more abundant, you can come and hit it from a different place.

I will say that when you start to expand (and this may be happening for some of you) any place where you have any type of darkness or unconsciousness – or any type of lack for that matter – it's going to come up and it's going to scream loudly at you because you're in the process of releasing it. And so, in order for it to be released and for the abundance and the light to come through, obviously it needs to be released. So the way it becomes released is if it comes and shows itself to you.

So while you go through this process, I want you to be really, really easy with yourself and kind to yourself. And if something comes up that you're noticing is going to sabotage you, or you're being cranky, judgmental (or whatever you want to call yourself), and you notice you're in a bad mood…just really connect with that and go back to that place of, "Am I feeling like I am enough?" Start with the core of who you are and really start feeling.

It's like going from lack to abundance. If you're feeling like, "I'm not enough," get in that feeling place of, "What would it be like if I did feel like I was enough? What would it feel like if I really were valuable?" Really get into that space and feeling like, "You know, I AM enough!"

Because I will tell you this: there is nothing on this planet that can add to you to make you more of who you are. You are enough. And it's been said by many, many spiritual, high-level beings that have walked the planet that there are about a thousand souls who want to take a body, but obviously only one gets that body.

So simply because of the fact that you are here in a physical body, you are enough. And that's all you really need to know. If you get that, then you know you are enough. You got the job, you're here, and this is your play. You are here to create what you want to create, this is your life to live, and it's a very short life in comparison to how eternal our being is. And if you can just get that you are enough and start feeling that you are enough and that you are valuable…once you get over that "Oh, I'm not enough" type of thing…then everything else flows.

Everything is about perspective. Changing your perspective will change your life. If you are resistant to sharing love, time, or anything you have with others, then you are in a space of lack. This perspective can always be shifted easily when you focus on abundance. Focus on what is right versus what is wrong in your life. That is the difference between an abundant mindset and a lack mindset.

I did my Goddess teleseminar and went over by 10 minutes. Someone emailed me and said, "You told us it would only be 60 minutes," and she was upset. Then I had an email from someone else who told me, "Wow, you gave so much more than you promised you would!" What is the difference? Perspective. One was in lack, focused on what was wrong. The other was focused on abundance and what was right.

Remember that every subject is really two subjects, and it is always your perspective of what makes it so. Change your perspective and your world changes.

Jerry Useem makes a good point in his article "Decisions Decisions" when he states: But there's a big difference between a wrong decision and a bad decision. A wrong decision is picking Door No. 1 when the prize is actually behind Door No. 2. It's a lousy result, but the fault lies with the method. A bad decision is launching the space shuttle Challenger when Morton Thiokol's engineers predict a nearly 100% chance of catastrophe. The method, in this case, is no method at all.

The distinction is important, because it separates outcomes, which you can't control, from process, which you can. Wrong decisions are an inevitable part of life. But bad decisions are unforced errors. They're eminently avoidable--and there are proven techniques to avoid the most predictable pitfalls (see "Great Escapes," page 97).

There is, of course, no one archetypical decision. Some are drawn out and deliberative, others made at the flick of a switch. If you find yourself at the receiving end of an Andy Roddick serve, for instance, pausing to weigh your options (forehand? backhand? law school?) is not an option. You have to jump, right now. For bond traders too, the time between analysis and action lasts milliseconds.

Now imagine you're responsible for a whole floor of bond traders. Orchestrated well, their decisions mean a great quarter; guided poorly, they'll dig a billion-dollar hole. You can't tell them what to decide, but you can train them how to decide, and select who does the deciding. That's how you build a decision-making machine--like GE or the Marine Corps. "If you explain to your subordinates the end state you want and the timeline you'd like to get there," says Gen. Peter Pace, "you can observe progress, provide resources, and know they're going to do things to get you to the goal. Maybe differently than you would do it. Often better. Sometimes worse. But inside the lines you've painted."

10

BAD GIRLS KNOW HOW TO SAY NO!

The real art of being a Bad Girl is to know when to say no!

You can do it too. It's an easy way to change your life without spending any of your money or time. Try to say no more often and enjoy these benefits:

1. You spend more time doing the things you want to do.

This is obvious, but it's also true. Don't feel guilty for saying no to something if you just can't bear the thought of it. Evaluate each situation separately.

For example, my friend explained that if a coworker she's not close to invites her to a baby shower, she says no immediately without guilt because she is better off with doing things she really wants to do.

Yet, she was candid enough to add that when her boss asks her to do something she takes a minute to think about how it will help her career before writing it off.

There are always things in life that you will have to do, but there should be some incentive for doing it, even if the act itself isn't exactly what you want to be doing in that moment. Don't place yourself second by catering to the things that are not in line with your future goals and overall happiness.

2. You weed out people who aren't important in your life.

By accepting invites and responsibilities only from people you truly care about, the less important ones tend to fade away.

Most people quickly realize that you don't have time for them and stop asking. Don't feel guilty; you simply can't spend quality time with the people you really care about if you divide your time among everyone that asks.

Don't be mean or rude; you don't want to create enemies, you just want to devote more time to people and activities you truly care about.

3. You get more out of your professional life.

When you say no to jobs and projects that don't fit in your professional goals, you are spending much more of your time on things that will get you where you want to be.

Choose colleagues and projects that offer you something, whether it is a fun environment or a topic that really interests you. You'll be much happier for it, and your career will soar because of it.

4. You are excited about your work.

By only doing work that you love, you can be excited about going to work. Being happy in your job increases productivity, which translates to a higher level of satisfaction. It is also a pathway to climb up the salary-ladder.

Money shouldn't be the only motivator of course, but unmotivated and unhappy employees don't get raises and promotions.

5. People respect you more when you say no.

We all know someone who we call a "sucker". You know who I'm talking about: The guy who does anything for anyone all the time. Everyone likes him because they can get what they want out of him, but no one has any respect for the guy or his time.

Don't be that guy. Do what is important to you. Let someone else be a sucker.

6. You get more out of your time.

If you're not at meetings you don't want to attend or at parties you feel pressured into going to, you can spend more time on a hobby you lost track of, or catch up with old friends who really mean a lot to you.

7. You are less stressed.

You know how you feel before you have to go to an event you really don't want to go to? The nervousness, the hurriedness, the overall feeling of stress? That goes away when you start saying "no" to these kinds of invites.

When stress is reduced, your overall health will get better. What can possibly be better than that?

8. People you care about thank you.

You will be a better spouse, parent, friend and colleague. People will appreciate you much more once you can give them your undivided attention. Your home life will be better, and your career will soar now that you can focus on doing things you love instead of always focusing on obligations.

Conclusions

I was always a people-pleaser because agreeing was always easier than saying no and feeling guilty. The reality, however, is that it's always easy to be a "yes" person until the time you can take it. That's when all the stress misery starts and it only continues the more time you waste on things that just don't matter.

Stop it right now by saying "NO" then next time someone asks you to do something that just doesn't fit in with your life goals. It will get easier, and the guilt will gradually go away.

An honest "no" will take you further than a superficial "yes".

Do you say "no" when you want to? How has it helped you?

11

BAD GIRL QUIZ

1. Have you ever kissed one of your friends' boyfriends?

Yes

No

2. Did you drink alcohol before you were 18?

Yes

No

3. Have you ever said mean things about your friends behind their backs?

Yes

No

4. Do you smoke?

Yes

No

5. Do you have any piercings below the neck?

Yes

No

6.   Have you ever shoplifted?

Yes

No

7.   Have you ever cheated on a boyfriend (kissing another guy counts here)?

Yes

No

8.   Have you ever spread lies or false rumors about someone?

Yes

No

9.   Have you ever picked a guy up at a party or bar?

10.   Have you ever flirted to get your way?

Yes

No

11.)   Have you ever bought anything from a sex shop?

Yes

No

12.) Have you ever kissed somebody of the same sex?

Yes

No

13.) Have you hit on a friend's boyfriend?

Yes

No

14.) Did you ever call somebody else's name while making out?

Yes

No

15.) Have you slept with over 40 men?

Yes

No

Answering yes to any of these questions makes you a bad girl. If you answered yes more than once then just add the word "very' in front of the word "bad" that number of times.

For instance; I am a very, very, very, very BAD girl!

12

MAE WEST - BAD GIRL QUOTES

"You only live once, but if you do it right, once is enough."

"I generally avoid temptation unless I can't resist it."

"There are no good girls gone wrong - just bad girls found out."

"I wrote the story myself. It's about a girl who lost her reputation and never missed it."

"Between two evils, I always pick the one I never tried before."

"When I'm good, I'm very good, but when I'm bad, I'm better. "

"Good sex is like good bridge. If you don't have a good partner, you'd better have a good hand."

"I'll try anything once, twice if I like it, three times to make sure."

"I'm no model lady. A model's just an imitation of the real thing."

"Don't cry for a man who's left you--the next one may fall for your smile."

"It's not the men in your life that matters, it's the life in your men."

"Ladies who play with fire must remember that smoke gets in their eyes."

"Sex is an emotion in motion."

"Too much of a good thing can be wonderful!"

"I'm single because I was born that way."

"Those who are easily shocked should be shocked more often."

"Cultivate your curves - they may be dangerous but they won't be avoided."

"I never worry about diets. The only carrots that interest me are the number you get in a diamond."

"It is better to be looked over than overlooked."

"Marriage is a great institution, but I'm not ready for an institution."

"Don't keep a man guessing too long - he's sure to find the answer somewhere else"

"I use to be Snow White, but I drifted."

"Women like a man with a past, but they prefer a man with a present"

"Look your best - who said love is blind?"

"All discarded lovers should be given a second chance, but with somebody else."

"Anything worth doing is worth doing slowly."

"Love thy neighbor -- and if he happens to be tall, debonair and devastating, it will be that much easier."

"I never said it would be easy, I only said it would be worth it."

"If a little is great, and a lot is better, then way too much is just about right!"

"His mother should have thrown him away and kept the stork."

"To err is human - but it feels divine."

"He who hesitates is a damned fool."

"Good women are no fun... The only good woman I can recall in history was Betsy Ross. And all she ever made was a flag."

"Good girls go to heaven, bad girls go everywhere."

"Is that a gun in your pocket, or are you just happy to see me?"

"You are never too old to become younger!"

"I have found men who didn't know how to kiss. I've always found time to teach them."

"Love conquers all things except poverty and toothache."

"Men are my hobby, if I ever got married I'd have to give it up."

"A dame that knows the ropes isn't likely to get tied up"

"Keep a diary and one day it'll keep you."

"I've no time for broads who want to rule the world alone. Without men, who'd do up the zipper on the back of your dress? "

"Every man I meet wants to protect me. I can't figure out what from."

"I've been things and seen places."

"A woman in love can't be reasonable--or she probably wouldn't be in love."

"The curve is more powerful than the sword."

"JUDGE: Are you trying to show contempt for this court?

MAE WEST: I was doin' my best to hide it."

"Everyone has the right to run his own life- even if you're heading for a crash. What I'm against is blind flying."

"One more drink and I'll be under the host."

"An ounce of performance is worth pounds of promises."

Epilogue

Well I have done my best to arm you with the most up to date and viable training on finding your inner Bad Girl. I hope you use these lessons well. There is nothing wrong with being a little naughty at times in fact as you well know by now it is actually quite therapeutic. So go on and live life unapologetically. You are a strong woman unafraid of showing her bad side, knowing that in the end, it's the Bad Girl who wins!